Explore!
AZTECS

D1332518

Izzi Howell

WAYLAND
www.waylandbooks.co.uk

Published in paperback in Great Britain in 2018
by Wayland

ISBN 978 1 5263 0060 7
10 9 8 7 6 5 4 3 2 1

Wayland
An imprint of Hachette Children's Group
Part of Hodder & Stoughton
Carmelite House
50 Victoria Embankment
London EC4Y 0DZ

An Hachette UK Company
www.hachette.co.uk
www.hachettechildrens.co.uk

A catalogue record for this title is available from the
British Library

Printed and bound in China

Produced for Wayland by
White-Thomson Publishing Ltd
www.wtpub.co.uk

Editor: Izzi Howell
Designer: Clare Nicholas
Picture researcher: Izzi Howell
Illustrations: Julian Baker
Wayland editor: Vicky Brooker
Consultant: Philip Parker

Picture acknowledgements:
The author and publisher would like to thank the
following agencies and people for allowing these
pictures to be reproduced:

Alamy Stock Photo/Art Archive 6; Alamy/Granger, NYC. 7;
Alamy Stock Photo/The Art Archive 10; Alamy Stock Photo/
North Wind Picture Archives 13 (bottom); Alamy Stock Photo/
Art Archive 14; Alamy Stock Photo/Art Archive 15 (top); Alamy
Stock Photo/Art Archive 17 (top); Alamy Stock Photo/Art
Archive 17 (bottom); Alamy Stock Photo/Art Archive 25 (top);
Getty/De Agostini 11 (top); iStock/Paolo_Toffanin cover (centr
right); iStock/stockcam title page (right) and 29; iStock/ghor-
nephoto 9 (bottom); iStock/Valenaphoto 12 (top left); iStock/
Images in the Wild 12 (top right); Library of Congress title page
(left) and 21 (bottom); Library of Congress 26; Shutterstock/
Vadim Petrakov cover (top right) and 22; Shutterstock/Anna
Omelchenko cover (bottom), 11 and 32; Shutterstock/Kapresk
icon; Shutterstock/Betacam-SP top line; Shutterstock/Michael
Vesia 4; Shutterstock/javarman 5 (bottom); Shutterstock/
Anna Biancoloto 12 (bottom left); Shutterstock/My name is bo
12 (bottom right); Shuttertock/Ondrej Prosicky 13 (centre);
Shutterstock/trekandshoot 15 (bottom left); Shutterstock/Leon
Rafael 16; Shutterstock/karamysh 18; Shuttestock/Chiyacat 19
(top); Shutterstock/cristalvi 19 (bottom); Shutterstock/Gordon
Galbraith 20; Shutterstock/Julio Aldana 21 (top); Shutterstock/
Everett Historical 27 (top); Shutterstock/Hugo Brizard – You-
GoPhoto 27 (bottom); Shutterstock/Nataliya Arzamasova 28;
Shutterstock/Leon Rafael 31; Werner Forman Archive/British
Museum, London cover (centre left); Werner Forman Archive/
Museum fur Volkerkunde, Vienna 5 (top); Werner Forman
Archive 9 (top); Werner Forman Archive/Liverpool Museum,
Liverpool, 13 (top), Werner Forman Archive/Museo Nazionale
Preistorico Etnografico Luigi Pigorini, Rome 15 (bottom right);
Werner Forman Archive/British Museum, London (Location:
29) 23 (top); Werner Forman Archive/Biblioteca Universitaria,
Bologna, Italy 23 (bottom); Wikimedia/Thelmadatter 8.

Design elements from Shutterstock.

Contents

Who were the Aztecs?

The Aztecs displayed their victims' skulls on a rack after they had been killed. This is a stone sculpture of an Aztec skull rack.

The Aztecs were an advanced Mexican civilisation that built magnificent cities. Through alliances with nearby states, they built up a massive army that dominated most of Mexico in the 15th and early 16th centuries.

Religion

Religion played an important role in the Aztec culture. The Aztecs believed that they had to sacrifice people to the gods regularly to keep the Sun moving across the sky. They often went to war with neighbouring states so that they would have prisoners of war to sacrifice in religious ceremonies.

Central American civilisations

The Aztecs were one of the last great civilisations in Central America. In the centuries before the Aztecs conquered most of Mexico, the land was controlled by groups such as the Maya, the Toltec and the Mixtec. The Aztecs traded with these groups and their descendants and shared ideas about religion.

This scene from an Aztec codex (book) shows two leaders having a meeting. It is drawn in a Mixtec style.

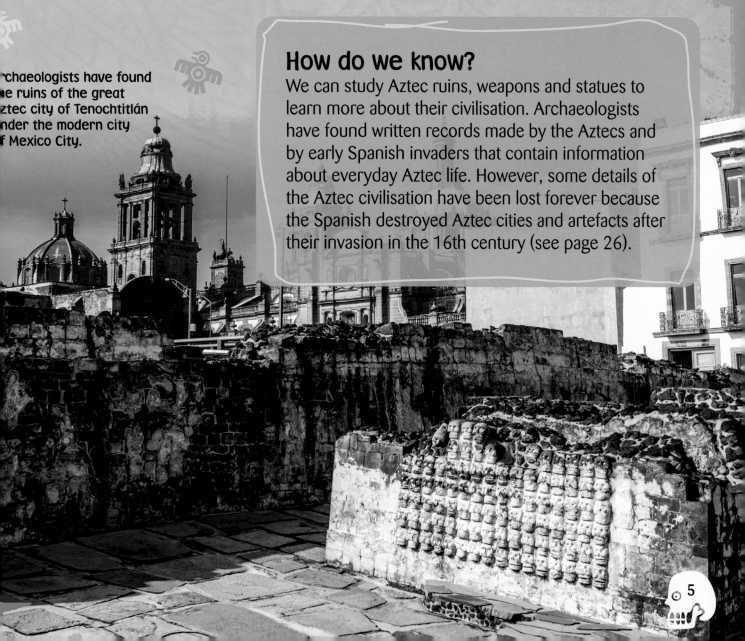

rchaeologists have found e ruins of the great ztec city of Tenochtitlán nder the modern city f Mexico City.

How do we know?

We can study Aztec ruins, weapons and statues to learn more about their civilisation. Archaeologists have found written records made by the Aztecs and by early Spanish invaders that contain information about everyday Aztec life. However, some details of the Aztec civilisation have been lost forever because the Spanish destroyed Aztec cities and artefacts after their invasion in the 16th century (see page 26).

The rise of the Aztecs

Within a few centuries, the Aztecs transformed themselves from a landless people to the rulers of most of central Mexico. Alliances with other powerful states gave them the strength to conquer and control many thousands of people.

Early legends

The first Aztecs moved from northern Mexico to central Mexico in around CE 1200. They struggled to find good farming land as most of central Mexico was already occupied. They kept moving around until they came across an island in Lake Texcoco in around 1325. They decided to build their home on the island after seeing what they believed to be a sign from their gods.

According to Aztec legend, the first settlers to arrive at Lake Texcoco saw an eagle sitting on a cactus with a snake in its mouth.

Gulf of Mexico

Lake Texcoco ○ Teotihuacan
Tlacopan ○ ○ Texcoco
○ Tenochtitlán

M E X I C O

▢ Aztec Territory

Pacific Ocean

A map of the Aztec territory around 1500.

Growing stronger

That first Aztec settlement on a marshy island soon became the city of Tenochtitlán. The Aztecs slowly became stronger and in 1372, they chose a ruler, or tlatoani, to control their expanding territory. In 1428, the Aztecs formed an alliance with two nearby states. The combined allied armies seized large areas of land and by the late 15th century, they had conquered most of Mexico, from the Pacific coast in the west to the Gulf of Mexico in the east.

City states and tribute

The Aztec tlatoani did not directly control every person in the Aztec territory. Most conquered lands were made up of city-states, which were governed by a local ruler. All city-states had to pay tribute to the Aztecs. They sent practical items, such as food and cloth, and valuable goods, such as tropical feathers and animal skins, to Tenochtitlán, the Aztec capital city.

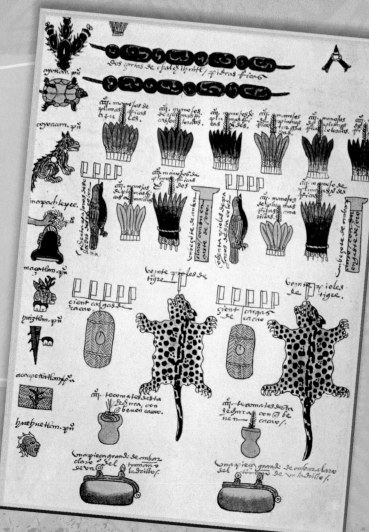

This Aztec codex shows some of the items offered as tribute, including jaguar skins, shields and feathers.

Aztec

society

This statue shows the tlatoani Itzcoatl, who ruled from 1426 to 1440. When a tlatoani died, a council of noblemen chose a new ruler from the remaining men in his family.

The tlatoani was at the top of Aztec society. Beneath him were city-state rulers, rich nobles, ordinary Aztecs and slaves.

The top of society

The Aztec tlatoani controlled the army and decided whether to conquer or form alliances with nearby states. His second-in-command was the cihuacoatl, who was in charge of the city of Tenochtitlán. The tlatoani Moctezuma I, who ruled from 1440 to 1469, introduced a rule that the tlatoani should only appear in public on very special occasions. He also made laws to differentiate noble people from ordinary people.

This Aztec jewellery is made from stone beads. Aztec noblemen and women also wore jewellery made from turquoise, gold, silver and shells.

Noblemen and women

The nobles were beneath the tlatoani in Aztec society. Noblemen were sent to special schools as children to train them to work in the government, army or priesthood. They were usually very rich and were allowed to wear expensive clothes and jewellery. Noblewomen lived a life of luxury, as they had slaves to carry out their household chores.

Ordinary people

Ordinary Aztecs made money by working as farmers, fishermen, merchants and craftsmen. They had to pay taxes to the tlatoani every year. In times of war, they were called up to fight with the Aztec army. Most ordinary Aztecs lived together in groups of families called calpolli. Each family had a separate house, but they worked and farmed together.

Families in a calpolli shared one piece of land for farming. They grew crops such as maize.

Cities and buildings

Very few Aztec cities and buildings can be seen today, as the Spanish destroyed most of them after their invasion. However, we have learned about Aztec construction from records and archaeological remains.

Tenochtitlán

The massive city of Tenochtitlán was the centre of the Aztec civilisation. It was built on an island in Lake Texcoco, with stone causeways that connected the city to the mainland. Tenochtitlán was filled with magnificent palaces, pyramids, canals and markets. Aqueducts brought fresh water from the mountains. Teams of cleaners worked to keep the city clean.

The Aztecs planned the construction of Tenochtitlán. Buildings were arranged in a grid with wide streets leading to the Great Temple.

Great Temple

At home

Most ordinary Aztecs lived in small houses made from adobe (dried clay) with thatched roofs. Inside, there was one room with separate areas for cooking, sleeping and eating. Most houses also had a small shrine to the gods, but ordinary people weren't allowed to decorate their houses in any other way. Noble Aztecs lived in stone houses, which were decorated with lavish ornaments and coloured cloth.

Aztec women were in charge of the cooking, cleaning and weaving, while men helped gather firewood and tended to the crops.

Teotihuacan

One of the most important places in the Aztec territory was the ruined city of Teotihuacan. This city was built hundreds of years before the Aztec civilisation and abandoned in the 8th century CE. However, its massive pyramids and avenues remained. The Aztecs decided that this was the site of the creation of the world.

Smaller pyramids line the avenue leading up to the 75-metre-high Pyramid of the Sun in Teotihuacan.

Trade and transport

The Aztecs traded goods across different regions in their territory and with other states. This allowed them to obtain valuable resources and other goods that they could not produce themselves.

At the market

Every Aztec town or village had its own marketplace, where local farmers and craftsmen sold their produce. However, the grandest marketplaces were in the cities of Tenochtitlán and Tlatelolco. Here, merchants sold products from all over Central America and even the southwest of the modern USA. Both ordinary people and nobles shopped at marketplaces. Instead of coins, they used cacao beans or cloth to pay for their purchases.

You could find anything from food, such as maize and quails, to shells and precious metals at an Aztec market.

This Aztec codex shows the god of merchants (left) carrying a crossroads decorated with merchants' footprints. On the right, there is a merchant carrying a cargo of quetzal birds.

Merchants

Aztec merchants were known as pochteca. They travelled across the Aztec territory and beyond, buying and selling goods. Their work was dangerous, as they often travelled with large amounts of valuable items. Unlike other Aztecs, they were allowed to enter enemy states to trade goods. Many pochteca acted as spies and brought back valuable information for the tlatoani.

Quetzal feathers were prized for their beauty by many central American civilisations, including the Aztecs.

Carrying goods

Although the Aztecs used wheels on children's toys, they didn't use them on carts for transportation. This is probably because there weren't any large animals suitable for pulling a cart in South America before the arrival of the Spanish in the early 16th century. Instead, the Aztecs carried goods in packs on their backs or transported them by boat.

Traders brought goods into the city of Tenochtitlán on flat-bottomed boats carved from tree trunks.

Weapons and war

The Aztecs were fierce warriors. They built and maintained their large territory by defeating neighbouring states in battle. Wars were common, as the Aztecs needed a constant supply of prisoners of war to sacrifice in their rituals.

Noble Aztec men dropping off their sons at the temple. Here, their sons will be trained as elite warriors.

Becoming a soldier

Every Aztec man had to serve in the army. At school, Aztec boys were taught to use weapons and defend themselves in battle. Later, these boys were sent to help in real wars by carrying weapons and assisting the warriors. Once they had experience, they were allowed to fight as well.

The Aztec army

The tlatoani was the leader of the Aztec army. Beneath him were professional warriors and ordinary men, who were called away from the fields to fight. Professional soldiers were often from noble families, but talented ordinary men could progress to this high-status position by capturing prisoners of war. As warriors became more skilled, their uniforms became more and more elaborate.

Eagle warriors were elite soldiers in the Aztec army. They wore beaked helmets, armour decorated with real feathers and claw-shaped spikes on their knees.

Wounding with weapons

Aztec warriors needed to capture live prisoners of war to sacrifice in their rituals so they used weapons to injure, rather than kill, their enemies. The Aztecs didn't have the technology to make metal weapons, so they made arrowheads and spearheads from obsidian, a hard black stone that can be made into a sharp blade. They also used obsidian blades on wooden swords, known as macuahuitl.

◄ An obsidian arrowhead. Archaeologists have found Aztec obsidian blades that are as sharp as a modern surgeon's knife.

◄ Aztec warriors used this device, known as an atlatl, to throw their spears over large distances.

15

Farming and food

The Aztecs needed a lot of food to support their large population. Their advanced farming techniques helped them to grow large amounts of crops, such as maize, but ordinary people often went hungry during droughts.

The Aztec diet

The ordinary Aztec diet was mainly vegetarian. The staple food was maize, which was ground into flour and made into porridge or tortillas (maize pancakes). The Aztecs also prepared vegetables such as beans, squash and tomatoes, which were often flavoured with spicy chillies. Aztec nobles ate grand meals with dozens of different meat and vegetable dishes. They drank a chocolate drink made from valuable cacao beans as a sign of their wealth and status.

Aztec women ground maize kernels into flour on stone metates (grinding slabs). This is a modern metate used today in Mexico.

On the farm

Aztec farmers grew crops such as maize, tomatoes, beans and squash. Some farmers also kept livestock, such as turkeys, ducks and rabbits. Ordinary people hunted wild birds and peccaries (small pigs) with bows and arrows and used nets and harpoons to catch fish. Any extra crops or meat could be sold in the markets.

The Aztecs stored dried maize in large bins so that they would have food to eat between harvests or during famines.

Terraces and islands

Aztec farmers used different farming techniques in different geographical areas. In the mountains, they built terraces with small stone walls to keep the soil from being washed away by rain. They dug ditches in dry areas to irrigate the soil. They also grew crops on chinampas – small artificial islands on lakes and swamps.

Chinampas were made from layers of reeds and fertile mud from the lake. The Aztecs planted trees around the edge of each island so that the tree roots would hold the island in place on the water.

A day in the life

Ordinary Aztec women spent most of their lives working at home. They cooked, cleaned and spun cloth while their husbands farmed or worked as craftsmen. This fictional diary entry describes a typical day in the life of an Aztec woman.

The bright light of the sun wakes me up early. I wake up the children and we make our way down to the lake to wash.

When we get back to the house, I sweep the floor. My eldest daughter and I take it in turns to tend the fire and grind maize into flour. We'll need the flour for our tortillas at lunch. I make a stew from tomatoes and chillies from the farm to serve alongside the tortillas.

Aztec women cooked maize tortillas on a hot stone placed over a fire. Today, some people in Mexico still prepare tortillas in the same way.

At midday, my husband comes back from the fields. He has been planting seeds and watering the crops all morning. I serve my family the stew in pottery bowls and we eat together.

Before I can start my afternoon chores, I light incense in our family shrine. I pray that the gods will give us a good harvest this year. It hasn't rained in a few weeks and I am worried that the crops will die without water.

I spend the afternoon weaving cloth on my loom, while my daughter spins cactus fibre into thread. The cactus threads are coarse but I know that I can make them into good cloth. If I have time before the sun sets, I will make some extra cloth to sell at the market next week.

To extract fibres from cactus leaves, the Aztecs scraped the flesh from the leaves and left them to dry in the sun. Then, they pulled the long fibres from the leaves.

Aztec women dyed cloth yellow using a natural pigment called ochre. They made red dye from insects that lived in cacti.

The diary entry on these pages has been written for this book. Can you create your own diary entry for another person that lived in an Aztec city? It could be a tlatoani or a travelling merchant. Use the facts in this book and other sources to help you write about a day in their life.

Religion
and beliefs

Religion played an important role in Aztec life. They worshipped many gods and regularly carried out sacrifices that they believed would make the gods happy.

Gods and goddesses

Each Aztec god or goddess represented a different area of everyday life. Some of the most important gods were Huitzilopochtli – god of war and the Aztec people, Tlaloc – god of rain and water, Quetzalcoatl – god of life and wind and Tezcatlipoca – god of justice and power.

Some Aztec gods were also worshipped by other civilisations. The original inhabitants of Teotihuacan worshipped a feathered serpent god, similar to the Aztec god Quetzalcoatl.

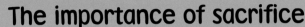

The importance of sacrifice

The Aztec religion was based on sacrifice (killing people as part of a ritual). They believed that their gods sacrificed themselves to create the Sun and make it move across the sky. The Aztecs thought that the Sun might stop rising and the world would end if they didn't continue to make sacrifices to the gods. They also hoped that the gods would give them good harvests and success in battle.

According to Aztec mythology, the Sun was created when the god, Huitzilopochtli, threw himself into a fire as a sacrifice.

In Aztec human sacrifices, a priest laid the victim on a special stone and then cut open the victim's chest with an obsidian knife. The priest removed the victim's heart and then let the body roll down the pyramid steps.

Human victims

Aztec priests carried out rituals and sacrifices in temples at the top of pyramids. Crowds of people gathered on the steps of the pyramids to watch these public ceremonies. Most sacrifice victims were prisoners of war, but certain ceremonies called for other types of victim, such as elderly women or children.

Art and writing

Aztec craftsmen produced large elaborate sculptures, beautiful jewellery and intricate written records. Talented craftsmen often made enough money to rise up through society and live a comfortable life.

Carving and sculptures

Aztec sculptors decorated the walls of temples and palaces with large carvings of religious scenes and figures. Small sculptures of the gods were made for the private shrines of noblemen. As the Aztecs didn't have the technology to create metal tools, they carved with stone tools.

This giant 3.7-metre-wide carving was found in the ruins of Tenochtitlán. It is decorated with glyphs and an image of the Aztec sun god Tonatiuh.

Luxury crafts

Many craftsmen focused on making luxury items from valuable resources such as precious stones and tropical feathers. Jade and turquoise were carved into masks and jewellery and brightly-coloured parrot feathers were made into headdresses. Decorated pottery was also popular.

This double-headed serpent decorated with turquoise was probably worn or carried by a priest during a religious ceremony. Snakes were a symbol of the god Quetzalcoatl.

This Aztec codex contains information about different days in the Aztec calendar. The Aztecs had a 260-day calendar and a 365-day calendar, which they borrowed from the Maya.

Glyphs and codices

The Aztec language, Nahuatl, did not have an alphabet. They used small pictures, called glyphs, to represent sounds and ideas. They added colours to their glyphs to add extra meaning, such as turquoise to represent a ruler. Aztec scribes kept records of important events and religious information in large books, called codices.

Make a patolli board game

The board game patolli was played by many groups of people across Central America, including the Aztecs. It was popular with both ordinary and noble people. Players often bet on the outcome of the game, offering food, cloth or valuable items to the winner. You can make your own patolli board and dice from cardboard and beans and learn how to play.

You will need:

cardboard

felt tip pen

10 dried beans, such as butter beans (or use a dice)

12 playing pieces (6 in one colour and 6 in another colour)

1

Cut out a patolli board as shown here. Mark the squares using a felt tip pen. Mark a dot on one side of each of the beans.

16cm

The rules of patolli

Each player is given five beans to use as dice. Roll the beans to decide who goes first. In order to place a playing piece on the board, a player must score a 1 (one bean landing dot side up) during the dice throw. Once a player has scored a 1, they can place one playing piece at their starting point.

The aim of the game is to get all of the playing pieces around all four arms of the board and out of play, by landing on the ending space. During their turn, each player rolls the dice. If they score a 1, they can move forward one space or add another playing piece to the board. If they score 2, 3 or 4, they must move forward that number of spaces. If they score a 5, they move forward ten spaces.

An Aztec illustration of two men playing patolli. The man on the right has bet some valuable feathers on the outcome of the game.

If a player lands on a triangle-shaped space or a semi-circular-shaped space, they get an extra turn. If a player lands on the same space as one of their opponent's pieces, they lose a turn. If both players land in the centre four squares at the same time, the second player to arrive must return their playing piece to the starting point.

Once a playing piece has reached the ending space, it cannot be taken by an opponent. The winner of the game is the player who gets their six playing pieces around the board and out of play first.

Handy hint

To make your patolli game more authentic, use coloured stones instead of playing pieces.

The end of the Aztecs

By the early 16th century, the Aztec civilisation had started to weaken. The Aztec territory was so large that it was hard for the tlatoani to keep control. Conquered states started to resent the Aztecs and the amount of tribute they had to provide.

Columbus and Cortés

After Christopher Columbus discovered the continent of North America in 1492, the Spanish sent conquistadors (conquerors) to explore and seize land in Central and South America. The conquistador Hernán Cortés arrived in Aztec territory in 1519. Before making his way to Tenochtitlán, he made alliances with the Aztecs' enemies, which added thousands of men to his army.

When the Spanish reached Tenochtitlán, Moctezuma II welcomed Cortés as a guest. However, as soon as Cortés was inside the palace, he took Moctezuma II hostage.

Fighting back

The Spanish started to take control of the city but they were stopped by an Aztec rebellion in June 1520. The Aztecs killed around three-quarters of the Spanish soldiers, but Moctezuma II also died in the fighting. The Spanish soldiers fled to safety. However, many of the surviving Aztecs in Tenochtitlán died from smallpox, a disease that the Spanish had brought to the Americas.

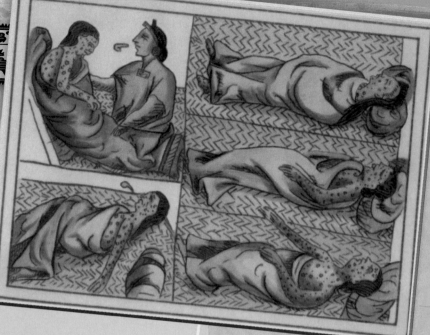

A huge number of Aztecs died from smallpox across Mexico. This made it much easier for the Spanish to take control of their lands.

Taking control

Cortés gathered a greater army, made up of Spanish soldiers and enemies of the Aztecs. They besieged Tenochtitlán and in August 1521, the Aztecs surrendered. The Spanish went on to seize all of the Aztec territory. They destroyed cities such as Tenochtitlán and forced the Aztecs to follow the Catholic religion and speak Spanish. However, some Aztecs survived. Today, their descendants speak a version of Nahuatl and remember their Aztec ancestors with pride.

The modern Mexican festival of the Day of the Dead has Aztec and Catholic origins. The original Aztec festival celebrated the goddess Mictecacihuatl, who looked after the bones of the dead.

Facts and figures

Some English words come from Nahuatl, the Aztec language. These words include tomato, shack, coyote, chocolate and avocado.

All Aztec children had to go to school until they were sixteen years old.

The Aztecs were named after Aztlán, which means 'white land'. This name probably refers to the area in the north of Mexico where the first Aztecs came from. The Aztecs also called themselves the Mexica. Later, this name turned into 'Mexico' and was used to describe the whole country.

The Aztecs ate large amounts of spirulina algae from Lake Texcoco. They gathered it from the lake using nets and made it into cakes. Today, spirulina is eaten as a health food, as it contains lots of vitamins and protein.

In 1518, just before the arrival of Cortés, there were up to 25.2 million people living in Aztec territory. By 1623, there were only around 700,000 native people in this area.

Over 4,000 prisoners of war were killed in the four-day-long ceremony to celebrate the opening of the Grand Temple in Tenochtitlán in 1487.

Timeline

CE 250–900	The Maya rule over an area of southern Mexico and Central America.
900s–1200s	The Toltec rule over central Mexico.
c.1200	The Aztecs arrive in central Mexico.
1325	After seeing a sign from their gods, the Aztecs settle on an island in Lake Texcoco.
1372	The Aztecs choose their first ruler, or tlatoani.
1428	The Aztecs grow stronger after forming an alliance with two nearby states.
late 1400s	The Aztecs control most of Mexico.
1519	The Spanish conquistador Hernán Cortés arrives in Aztec territory and starts to take control.
1521	The Aztecs surrender to the Spanish.

Glossary

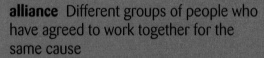

alliance Different groups of people who have agreed to work together for the same cause

ancestors People from your family who lived a long time ago

aqueduct A structure for carrying water across land

archaeologists People who learn about the past by digging up old objects

artefact An object from the past that reveals information about the people who made it

besiege To surround a place with an army in order to attack it

cacao A tropical tree that has seeds that can be made into chocolate

causeway A raised road over a wet area

CE The letters 'CE' stand for 'common era'. They refer to dates from CE 1.

city-state A state made up of a city and the area surrounding it, often ruled by one leader

civilisation A well-organised society

codex (codices) Written Aztec records

conquistador One of the Spanish people that travelled to Central and South America in the 16th century and seized the land from native people

drought A long period where there is little or no rain

elite Describes a person who belongs to the most important group in a society

fertile Describes land in which you can grow good-quality crops

fictional Made-up or invented

glyph A symbol used to represent a sound or a word in the Aztec written language

incense A substance that burns with a strong sweet smell

jade A precious green stone

merchant A person who travels around buying and selling goods

noble The richest, most-powerful people in a society, second only to the king

obsidian A glassy rock formed when volcanic lava cools

pigment A substance that gives something else a colour when it is added to it

resource Things such as rocks and wood that can be found in an area and used by people.

ritual A religious ceremony where certain actions are carried out

sacrifice The act of killing an animal or a person because you believe it will make a god happy

scribe Someone who writes and reads documents

shrine A place or building where people offer prayers and gifts to gods

territory An area of land that is ruled by a particular leader or group of people

tribute Payment made by a conquered city-state to the ruler of the Aztecs, usually in the form of valuable goods

valuable Describes something that is very useful or worth a lot of money

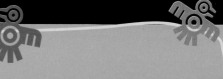

Further reading

The Aztecs (At Home With…),
Tim Cooke (Wayland, 2016)

The Aztecs (Gruesome Truth About),
Jillian Powell (Wayland, 2012)

**The Maya and other American Civilisations
(Technology in the Ancient World),**
Charlie Samuels (Franklin Watts, 2015)

Websites

http://www.dkfindout.com/uk/history/aztecs/
An in-depth guide to the Aztecs, illustrated with drawings and photos.

http://www.bbc.co.uk/schools/primaryhistory/worldhistory/double_headed_serpent/
Learn more about the history of the double-headed serpent statue on page 24.

http://www.bbc.co.uk/education/clips/zxmxpv4
Watch a video about the excavation of the ruins of Tenochtitlán in Mexico City.

http://www.ducksters.com/history/aztec_empire/tenochtitlan.php
Find out more information about the magnificent Aztec capital city of Tenochtitlán.

Index